GOING WEST!

A WILLIAMSON *KALEIDOSCOPE KIDS®* BOOK

DEDICATION

To our grandmother, Louise Johmann, who told us tales of coming to America, and to all the pioneers who struggled to settle this country. Their spirit lives on today.

ACKNOWLEDGMENTS

Many thanks to Diana Carter of the Cincinnati Public Library, Jim Dierks of the New York Museum of Transportation, Gail Fines of the National Frontier Trails Center, Thomas Grasso of the Canal Society of New York State, Martha Johnson of the Genesee Country Village and Museum, and Mark Koziol of the Erie Canal Museum for sharing their expertise and historical perspective; to librarians Roxanne Chadwick, Joan Parlato, Sandra Schumacher, and Eileen Sheridan for reviewing our list of resources; to John, Courtney, and Jessica for their help and encouragement; and to two pioneers of the new millennium — Christine and David — for checking out canals and building forts.

Williamson Books by
Carol A. Johmann and Elizabeth J. Rieth
***Bridges!* Amazing Structures to Design, Build & Test**

GOING WEST!

JOURNEY ON A WAGON TRAIN TO SETTLE A FRONTIER TOWN

Carol A. Johmann & Elizabeth J. Rieth

Illustrations by Michael Kline

WILLIAMSON PUBLISHING • CHARLOTTE, VT

Library of Congress Cataloging–in–Publication Data

Johmann, Carol, 1949–
    Going West! : journey on a wagon train to settle a frontier town / Carol A. Johmann & Elizabeth J. Rieth; illustrations by Michael Kline.
        p. cm.— (A Kaleidoscope Kids® book)
    Includes index.
    Summary: Describes the choices and decisions the pioneers faced as they traveled to the American West and built settlements there. Includes activities.
    ISBN 1-885593-38-4
    1. Frontier and pioneer life—West (U.S.)—Study and teaching—Activity programs—Juvenile literature. 2. Pioneers—West (U.S.)—History—19th century—Study and teaching—Activity programs—Juvenile literature. 3. Overland journeys to the Pacific—Study and teaching—Activity programs—Juvenile literature. 4. West (U.S.)—History—1848–1860—Study and teaching—Activity programs—Juvenile literature. 5. West (U.S.)—Social life and customs—19th century—Study and teaching—Activity programs—Juvenile literature. [1. Frontier and pioneer life—West (U.S.) 2. Overland journeys to the Pacific. 3. West (U.S.)—History.] I. Rieth, Elizabeth, 1957– II. Kline, Michael P., ill. III. Title. IV. Series.

F593.J58 2000
978'.02—dc21
                                    99-089622

Photography: page 10: *The Trail of Tears*, **Woolaroc Museum**, Bartlesville, Oklahoma; page 16 (poster): **Library of Congress**, LC-USZ62-407-87; page 18 (homesteaders): #2938, page 61 (Sylvester Rawding family): #1784, and page 87 (the Chrisman Sisters): #1053, SD Butcher, pages 5 and 60 (gathering cow chips): #1072, **Nebraska State Historical Society**; page 21: *Handcart Pioneers*, **Intellectual Reserve, Inc.**, **Courtesy of Museum of Church History and Art**, **Used by Permission**; page 66 (McGuffey's Reader): **Ohio Historical Society**. Artwork from **PicturesNow.com**, San Rafael, California: cover (background art), pages 3, 5, 19, 31, 53, 55, 57, 58, 63, 65, 70, 76, 83, and 84.

Kaleidoscope Kids® series editor: **Susan Williamson**
Cover and interior design: **Black Fish Design**
Designers: **Danny Yee, Joseph Lee, Sue Yee, Daniella Chadwick, Erich Lazar**
Illustrations: **Michael Kline**
Printing: **Quebecor Printing, Inc.**

Printed in Canada

Williamson Publishing Co.
Box 185
Charlotte, Vermont 05445
1-800-234-8791

10 9 8 7 6 5 4 3 2 1

CONTENTS

A NATION OF MOVERS

Almost half a million Americans moved west along trails such as the Oregon Trail and the Santa Fe Trail in the mid-1800s. That's a lot of moving. But when you think about it, the United States always had been a nation of movers. After all, most Americans — or their parents or grandparents — had come here from Europe to seek a better life or freedom of religion. It was natural for them to consider moving when they wanted to own land, earn more money, or just be free in wide open spaces. Yes, moving west was in the very nature of the early American tradition of individuality and independence.

The earliest colonists started this trend when they left their settlements on the Atlantic Coast and moved into the wild western regions of the colonies. A few generations later, Americans like Daniel Boone pushed their way into the backwoods of Kentucky and Tennessee. Then, others moved into Alabama and Mississippi, western New York, and the upper valley of the Ohio River. By the 1820s, American boys and girls were growing up hearing about Oregon, California, and Texas. They became the generation that pushed the American frontier all the way to the Pacific Ocean.

Movin' and Groovin'

Americans are a mix of people from all over the world. Interview your parents and grandparents to find out where they came from. Once they were in America, did they move around a lot? Did your ancestors travel on the western trails in the 1800s? See just how "movin' and groovin'" earlier generations of Americans were. Look to the four W's to help you in your quest:

- ***Who** came to the United States?*
- ***When** did they come, and **how** did they get here?*
- ***Why** did they leave their original homelands?*
- ***Where** did they settle?*

P.S. If you don't live with your birth family, find out where the people you live with came from — as far back as you can discover.

P.P.S. If you are lucky enough to have some relatives, friends, or neighbors in their 80s, 90s, or even 100 years old, ask them if you can tape or videotape an interview with them about their parents, grandparents, sisters, and brothers. You'll be recording history!

The Bargain of a Lifetime!

If you look at a map of the U.S. today, you can see that the land east of the Mississippi River makes up about a third of the country (minus Alaska and Hawaii). With the signing of the *Louisiana Purchase*, the size of the U.S. in 1803 more than doubled! This great expanse of land was now open to Americans for exploration, fur trade, timber, and eventually settling and farming. In addition, the important port of New Orleans at the mouth of the Mississippi was included in the deal.

That's an awful lot to get for just $15 million, but that's what President Thomas Jefferson agreed to pay France. Although it was a good price, it was more money than the U.S. Treasury had, so the government had to borrow money from Britain to pay France. Even so, the Louisiana Purchase is one of the greatest land bargains in all of history. No blood was spilt obtaining it, and each acre cost only three pennies. Imagine getting a whole acre of land for just three cents!

Think About It!

Is This Land My Land?

What does *owning* land mean? What does it mean to be a *steward* (protector) of the land? Consider the U.S. National Parks. As U.S. citizens, we pay taxes to buy parkland and maintain it, but does that mean we "own" the parks? Or are we the land's protectors, having the right to enjoy the land and what's on it as long as we don't disturb it? Ask your parents about any property they might own. Do they have the right to do anything with it, or are there restrictions?

Thomas Jefferson

A CLASH OF CULTURES

For all its seeming emptiness, North America was already occupied when the first Europeans arrived and started exploring and moving west. About 300 different nations (tribes) of Native American Indians lived on the North American continent, some for thousands of years. Some of them stayed in one place, building villages and farming. Other nations were nomadic, moving in search of buffalo and other animals to hunt.

Different Indian nations often fought with each other, just as nations around the globe still do today. But they all agreed on one thing: They called the earth their Mother. It was something the Creator, or Great Spirit, had made. It belonged to everyone. *No one person could own the land.*

Europeans and Americans had a different point of view. As soon as the Pilgrims had arrived, they began to divide the land and put up fences. All the pioneers that followed did the same thing. For them, land was something to own, to tame, and to settle. The Indians could not understand this. How could a person own the earth and the animals and plants on it? This basic difference between the cultures led to conflicts from the start, and it only got worse as time went on. Even today, there are disagreements over who owns the land in some parts of the United States.

"We were content to let things remain as the Great Spirit made them. They (white men) were not, and would change the rivers and mountains if they did not suit them. We were like deer. They were like grizzly bears."

Chief Joseph, Nez Perce

THE TRAIL OF TEARS

Perhaps more than any other nation, the *Cherokee* in Georgia tried to adapt to the culture of the new settlers. They created an alphabet, established schools, churches, and farms, and generally adopted the white man's ways. They even accepted the idea of individuals owning land. Then, in 1830, the U.S. government passed the *Indian Removal Act.* The law said that the government no longer had to recognize old treaties that gave Indian nations east of the Mississippi River the right to their homelands. The state of Georgia immediately claimed Cherokee land.

Helped by white supporters, the Cherokee nation went all the way to the Supreme Court to fight the state. The court decided in the Indians' favor, but Georgia ignored the decision. Other southern states quickly followed Georgia's example. Over the next few years, the Cherokee, *Creek*, and other nations were forced to leave their home- lands and move to Indian Territory in Oklahoma. Some left in the middle of a drought, when water and food were scarce. Others traveled without blankets or shoes in one of the coldest winters the South had ever seen. Thousands died along the way. They called the path they took the *Trail of Tears.*

The Trail of Tears *by Robert Lindneux, 1942*

general stores, blacksmiths, wagon-makers, harness-makers, and gunsmiths. Kids like us are being hurried along by anxious parents. Large pens hold horses, mules, and oxen for sale. It's hard to imagine that each wagon train can hold from 20 to 300 families' possessions, plus everything they'll need for the six-month journey ahead!

The streets of Independence, deep in mud from the spring rains, are crowded with all sorts of people — mountain men in buckskin, Indians in blankets, Mexicans with big straw hats, merchants in tall beaver hats, and, of course, all us pioneer-types in our sturdy wool clothes.

But we don't have time to mosey around and get acquainted with the place. We arrived a bit late because we had to wait for the ice on the canal to melt, and we've only a few short weeks to get our wagon ready. The grass on the prairies has just begun to grow and turn green this early spring. The wagons will leave when there's enough grass for the livestock to eat. There's no time to dawdle.

CONESTOGAS AND PRAIRIE SCHOONERS

The Oregon Trail was more than 2,000 miles (3,200 km) long, with about half of it going through mountains. Large freight wagons like the *Conestogas* that people used back East and along the Santa Fe Trail to the Southwest were too heavy for animals to pull across the great distance of the Oregon Trail, and they were too wide for the narrow mountain passes. (And most farm wagons were just plain too rickety to hold up over the rough trails.)

If an emigrant could afford one, the *prairie schooner* was the best wagon. Half the weight of a Conestoga, and only 4' x 12' (1.2 x 3.7 m), it was light enough for a team of oxen or mules to pull, yet sturdy enough to carry 2,500 pounds (1,125 kg). A wooden frame, tall enough for a man to stand under, held up the white canvas cover that was waterproofed with linseed oil. The cover could be drawn closed at both ends to protect against wind, rain, or dust, or rolled back to let a breeze through.

Prairie schooner

Conestoga wagon

A SEA OF GRASS

Pioneers often painted their wagons blue and the wheels red. With their white covers, the wagons must have been a patriotic sight. But in the sea of tall grass at the start of the trail, the blue wagons and red wheels were hidden. Only the white tops billowing in the wind like sails on a ship could be seen. That's why people nicknamed the wagons "prairie schooners" after the large sailing ships called schooners.

YOU ARE THERE

Our Own Wagon!

Pa, of course, selected a prairie schooner for our journey. He looked nervous as he counted out $100 to buy the schooner. We had planned to save money and build our own wagon, but we don't have enough time. Our wagon sure is a beauty. Ma likes its bright, white cover. It looks so big, but when we all pile in (without our supplies!), it is clear we'll be doing a lot of walking alongside.

Think About It!

Working Together

Big decisions are difficult for every family, and often they revolve around money — and how to use it. Should we buy a new car or try to fix the old one again? Should we move to a bigger apartment? Can we go to that special restaurant to celebrate? Can we buy a used piano?

Back in the 1840s or so, "Pa" was the decision-maker, but today things are much different. Moms are equal partners in the decision-making, and in many families, kids have a lot of input, too.

If you had more to say in family decisions, do you think you'd help more to make them work out well? Ask your folks if you can join in the effort — families working together! It makes hard work and sacrifice for a common goal fun!

Build Your Prairie Schooner

Supplies

- Large, rectangular cardboard box for wagon bed
- Scissors
- Cardboard (for wheels)
- 4 paper fasteners
- 4 pieces of long, thin balsa wood [$1/32$" x 2" x 36" (.625 mm x 5 cm x 90 cm) works well]
- Masking tape
- Paintbrushes
- Red and blue tempera paints, in dishes or lids
- Rope
- Old white sheet or pillowcase
- String

1. *Remove the top of the box. Cut out four wheels and attach them to the box using the paper fasteners.*

2. *To make the frame for the wagon's cover, gently bend a piece of balsa wood, so the ends fit inside the wagon sides. Tape the ends in place. Repeat with the other pieces.*

3. *Paint the wheels red and the wagon blue.*

4. *Tie the rope all around the sides of the wagon.*

5. *Cut the sheet or pillowcase to the right size for your wagon. It should hang slightly over the frame of the wagon all the way around.*

6. *Make some holes along all the edges of the material. On the two long sides, thread one piece of string through each hole. Tie the sides of the cover to the rope. At each end, thread a string through all the holes; then, use the strings like a drawstring to close the cover at both ends and tie it to the rope.*

EVERYTHING YOU EVER WANTED TO KNOW ABOUT ...

Guidebooks like *The Emigrants Guide to Oregon and California, Horn's Overland Guide,* and *Journal of Travels Over the Rocky Mountains* explained how to outfit wagons and how much food to bring. They included maps and described landmarks along the trail. They even listed the best river crossings and places to camp! The books also showed pictures of animals and plants found along the trail, indicating which plants and berries were safe to eat. (Many pioneers who didn't pay attention got sick and even died from eating poisonous plants.)

Oxen or Mules?

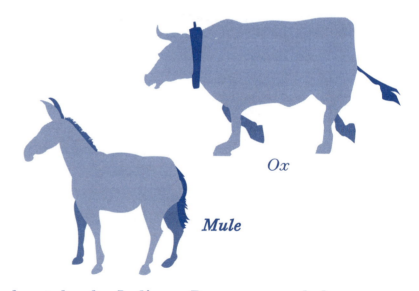

Ox

Mule

The emigrants argued all the time over oxen versus mules. Mules are faster, so gold rushers often used them. But mules could be stubborn, stopping for no reason and refusing to go on. (Ever hear the expression "stubborn as a mule"? Guess where it came from!) Mules also were nervous and sometimes ran away from loud noises like a gunshot or a clap of thunder. Plus, to keep strong and healthy, mules needed grain to eat, and grain took up precious space in the wagons and cost money.

Oxen, on the other hand, cost half the price of mules and were steadier and more obedient. One ox could pull almost as much as two mules. Plus, oxen could get through mud better, stay strong eating only grass, and were less likely to be stolen by Indians. But oxen needed more time to feed, so they couldn't work as many hours in a day as mules could.

So make your choice — oxen or mules? Four oxen or six mules usually are the fewest that can do the job. Considering that the trip is going to be as hard on them as it will be on you, having a few spare beasts of burden might be a good idea. Think about how many you would buy.

MA, WE'RE STARVING!

Covered wagons had no refrigerators, no ice-boxes, no coolers. Yet, the pioneers had to bring enough food to last for months. Some foods like flour and sugar weren't a problem because they don't spoil in hot weather. Other foods like fruits, vegetables, and meat went bad within days. What did the pioneers do? They dried meats and fruits, preserved foods like pickles and potatoes in salt, and harvested fresh berries, nuts, fish, and meat from nature along the way. But it wasn't exactly a picnic — and, yes, it took very careful planning.

Dry It, You'll Like It!

Gather up some juicy, tart apples. With an adult's help, remove the skin and cores. Cutting crosswise, make thin donut-shaped slices. String the slices like a necklace and hang them up to dry. Drying may take a day or two, depending on the season and how thin your slices are. When they're ready, the slices will be dry, brown, and leathery.

Once dry, store them in air-tight containers. Try adding dried vegetables to soups and stews — just like they did on the trail. Yum!

Outfitting Our Wagon

Pretend you're helping Pa. Our family has six people in it, and Pa has $700 left in his pocket after buying our wagon, so we visit the pens to buy some oxen. (Yes, Pa's decided on oxen because they cost less, and we don't have money or room for grain.) Oxen work in pairs connected by a wooden yoke, and each pair with its yoke costs Pa $75.

Our next stop is the general store. It's loaded with things to buy. After reading our guide-books, we know we need lots of flour, corn-meal, salt, bacon, beans, rice, and sugar. And coffee, syrup, pickles, lard, and crackers, too! The amount for our family adds up to $90 and weighs a whopping 1,200 pounds (540 kg)!

How much money does Pa have left in his pocket? How much more weight can our wagon hold? From the choices on the next page, please help us decide what other supplies to buy, adding up the cost and weight as you go along. Remember, our family needs not only enough supplies to last five to six months on the trail, but also tools, supplies, and some cash to set up our new farm once we arrive in Oregon. Please keep in mind that we have brought some things with us to Independence. They won't cost us anything now, but we do have to con-sider their weight. So what else should we buy? We're counting on your thoughtful plan-ning (and, since you're a kid like me, I know you'll remember to sneak in a few tiny, "weightless" treats)!

YOU ARE THERE

Don't Forget!

- Our wagon can hold about 2,500 pounds (1,125 kg).
- Though they may not be our favorites, fruits and vegetables are important so we don't get scurvy (a disease caused by lack of vitamin C).
- We need to save some money for purchases at forts along the way and for use when we reach our new home.

Belongings We Brought from Home

treasure trunk (empty)	45 lbs/20.25 kg
rocking chair	8 lbs/3.5 kg
set of china	40 lbs/18 kg
grandfather clock	65 lbs/29.25 kg
fiddle	3 lbs/1.5 kg
harmonica	*
stone jars filled with butter	15 lbs/6.75 kg

Tools and Equipment

	Price	Weight
30 feet (9.25 m) of rope	.60	2 lbs/1 kg
30 feet (9.25 m) of chain	1.60	33 lbs/14.75 kg
canteen	.35	*
water barrel	1.00	4 lbs/2 kg
pail	.50	3 lbs/1.25 kg
pickax	1.00	4 lbs/2 kg
shovel	1.00	5 lbs/2.25 kg
ax	1.00	5 lbs/2.25 kg
hatchet	.80	3 lbs/1.25 kg
anvil	10.00	100 lbs/45 kg
nails	.05	1 lb/.50 kg
jar of axle grease	.10	10 lbs/4.5 kg
plow	8.90	70 lbs/31.5 kg

Spare Wagon Parts

	Price	Weight
wagon cover	7.50	9 lbs/4 kg
yoke	4.50	25 lbs/11.25 kg
axle	7.50	20 lbs/9 kg
tongue (a type of beam)	8.50	35 lbs/15.75 kg
wheel	10.00	10 lbs/4.5 kg

Clothing

	Price	Weight
1 set of clothing	1.00	6 lbs/2.75 kg
1 pair of boots	2.00	8 lbs/3.5 kg
1 pair of shoes	1.00	3 lbs/1.25 kg
hat	1.00	*
long underwear	.50	3 lbs/1.25 kg
raincoat	2.90	3 lbs/1.25 kg
heavy coat	10.00	5 lbs/2.25 kg
mittens	.60	1 lb/.50 kg
blanket	2.00	6 lbs/2.75 kg

Food and Equipment

	Price	Weight
ham	1.50	10 lbs/4.5 kg
sack of potatoes	.40	20 lbs/9 kg
sack of onions	.90	10 lbs/4.5 kg
tin of preserved potatoes	.25	5 lbs/2.25 kg
cheese	.30	1 lb/.50 kg
sack of dried fruit	.30	5 lbs/2.25 kg
sack of dried vegetables	.20	5 lbs/2.25 kg
candy	.80	1 lb/.50 kg
coffee mill	.45	3 lbs/1.25 kg
coffee pot	.35	1 lb/.50 kg
frying pan	.25	5 lbs/2.25 kg
set of eating utensils	.85	4 lbs/2 kg
set of cooking utensils	4.00	27 lbs/12 kg
pots	.90	5 lbs/2.25 kg
kettle	.90	7 lbs/3 kg
Dutch oven (large soup pot)	1.55	10 lbs/4.5 kg
cookstove	16.00	260 lbs/117 kg

Livestock (to be bought in Independence)

	Price	Weight
milk cow	15.00	will walk
chicken	3.00	4 lbs/2 kg

General Supplies

	Price	Weight
mirror	.10	3 lbs/1.25 kg
1 dozen candles	1.20	4 lbs/2 kg
lantern	.45	2 lbs/1 kg
tin of lantern oil	.80	1 lb/.50 kg
box of matches	.25	*
fishing pole, hook & line	.80	*
keg of gunpowder	5.50	25 lbs/11.25 kg
rifle	20.00	5 lbs/2.25 kg
box of 20 bullets	1.80	10 lbs/4.5 kg
shotgun	20.00	7 lbs/3 kg
box of 10 bars of soap	.50	6 lbs/2.75 kg
washboard	.35	2 lbs/1 kg
box of medicinal supplies	1.85	5 lbs/2.25 kg

When no weight is shown, the item weighs less than 1 pound (.5 kg).

HOW GOOD WERE YOUR CHOICES?

The success of the pioneers' journey depended on the supplies they brought with them. Plain and simple: Poor planning could mean death from starvation or wagon breakdown. Let's see how good your decisions were.

How many oxen did you buy? Only two yoke (two pairs)? That might not be enough, because one or two oxen are likely to die of exhaustion before you reach Oregon. Three or four yoke (6 or 8 oxen) is a better choice.

How about spare wagon parts? Wheels and axles often break on the trail. Sometimes they can be fixed, but what will happen if they can't be, and you don't have a spare?

What about food? Did you buy a lot of fresh potatoes? Not a good idea. They'll take up a lot of room in your wagon. How about meat? If you bought too much, it probably will spoil — along with the potatoes — before you reach the first fort. Did you remember to pack a rifle or shotgun along with enough ammunition so you can hunt for fresh game along the way?

And what about fresh eggs and milk for the children? You did remember to buy a cow and some chickens, didn't you? It's a lot better to have a cow along than to bring those heavy jars of butter. They'll just weigh you down. And the butter will probably spoil before too long

I simply REFUSE to walk!

anyway. Plus, you can make trail butter along the way if you have a cow (see page 64).

What about your personal items? Did you buy extra blankets and coats or bring them from home? Good. It gets mighty cold on the trail. Did you keep your furniture and china? They'll only weigh down the wagon, and they'll probably break when the wagons are driven across rivers or up mountains. Still, most people bring them along. It's hard to part with precious family heirlooms.

So, how did you do? Did you make good choices? If not, go back and refigure space, weight, and supplies before the wagon train sets out. There's still time to get the family properly equipped.

Think About It!

To Have and to Hold

Prairie schooners left Independence filled to the brim. Every bit of space inside and out of the wagon was used. But so much had to be left behind. Just as the grown-ups had to part with their favorite belongings, so did the children.

Take a look around your room. Is it overflowing with toys, books, stuffed animals, and games? Imagine you're with your present-day family and setting out on the trail to Oregon. You can choose one thing to take with you, and it must be *small*. How will you decide? Will you bring your favorite toy? The book you love to read? The cuddly bear that helps you sleep? It's a tough choice.

Make a Trunk for Your Treasures

Make a trunk for your secret treasures from a shoebox that has a lid. You'll also need scissors, three paper fasteners, gift wrap, some fabric scraps, and glue. Remember: If it doesn't fit, it doesn't make the trip!

Cut the two corners on one long side of the lid as shown. Make three holes in that side and three matching holes along the top of one long side of the box. Use the paper fasteners to connect the lid to the box. Line the inside of the box with the gift wrap. Decorate the outside, too. Use a brown paper bag or brown fabric to make it look like leather, or make it more colorful by gluing on fabric or construction paper.

Now pack some treasures in your trunk and store it on the bottom of your wagon, near the center where the heavy stuff belongs.

YOU ARE THERE

Big Train or Little Train?

Like most Americans, we pioneers like doing things on our own, and Pa is no different. But going it alone on the trail is foolhardy. So just about everyone — including us — joins a wagon train. Some people choose to travel with just a few other families. Others join trains of hundreds of wagons. What are we going to do? Before deciding, Ma and Pa are considering this:

Small groups are nice because you get to know and trust everyone. And they move faster, too. A dozen wagons can cross a river in much less time than two hundred wagons. On the other hand, large wagon trains often have an experienced scout or wagon master. Moreover, with more people, an accident or illness is less likely to wipe out so many people that the others are left stranded, unable to get the wagons through the mountains.

Knowing our ma and pa (in this book), what do you think they decided to do — small group or large?

Think About It!

Personal Comfort

Imagine what your own mom and dad would have chosen to do, and then imagine which situation you personally would have preferred. Would you have been happier with 12 families or with 200 families? Consider your personality and your feelings about safety in making your decision.

Traveling the Trail

Pa's assigned you the job of keeping track of landmarks on the map because he knows you have a good sense of direction. He tells you to study the map hard and know it like "the back of your hand" before we start out. Do you spy a prairie dog? Where will you carve your name? Try to find each of the places and things written in bold type below, so you'll be able to alert your family to the sights and dangers as you pass by.

5 Here is where the trail split. Those heading for **Oregon** headed northwest, through the canyons of the twisting **Snake River** and across the **Blue Mountains** to the **Columbia River**. The Columbia spills over a **waterfall** into a deep gorge. One treacherous way to get to the valley was down the rapids on rafts and Indian canoes. Another way was over the **Barlow Road** through the **Cascade Range**. This was a dangerous route, too, with steep hills and narrow passes.

6 Those bound for **California** headed southwest across the **Nevada** desert. Animals died of heat and exhaustion, and their skeletons littered the trail. Then, the wagons had to be hoisted up the **Sierra Nevadas** and down the tree-covered slopes to **San Francisco** and **Sacramento**. To get to **Utah**, the Mormons went directly south after **Fort Bridger** and headed to the **Great Salt Lake** in Utah.

4 **Devil's Gate** pointed the way to **South Pass**, a valley through the **Continental Divide** that marked the halfway point (hooray!) and the beginning of the **mountains**. The trail dipped down to **Fort Bridger** and then up again to **Fort Hall**. At nearby **Soda Springs**, emigrants stopped and stocked up on bicarbonate — nature's own baking soda.

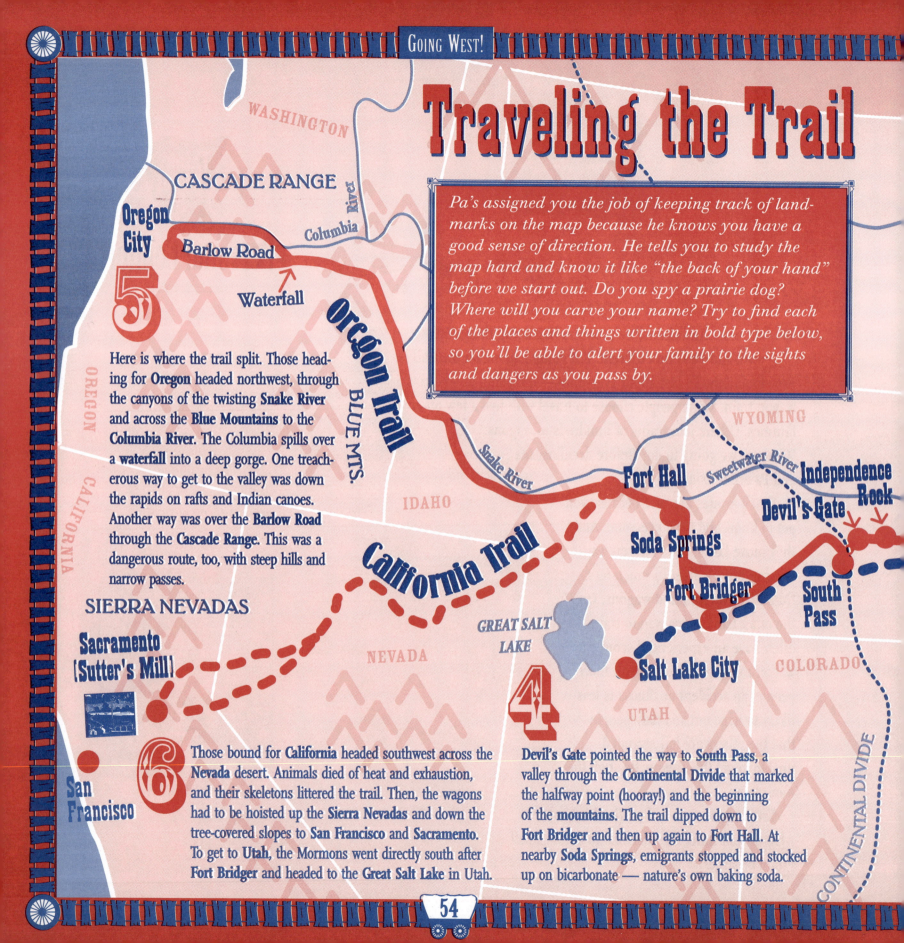

3

As the land started to rise, strange shapes appeared — rocky landmarks like **Chimney Rock** that looked like a house with a chimney and **Scotts Bluff** that resembled a medieval castle. The trading post at **Fort Laramie** came just in time. By then, the pioneers needed a rest and more supplies. After that came the **Sweetwater River** and the whale-shaped **Independence Rock** known as the great register because many pioneers climbed it to paint or carve their names.

2

Next came the **Platte rivers.** The "Old Muddy," as the pioneers called it, was said to be "a thousand miles long and six inches deep." As the wagons moved west, the air became drier and the grass shorter and brown. The sun scorched your skin. Funny little **prairie dogs** popped out of the sandy soil among the prickly pear cactus. Huge herds of buffalo — each with maybe thousands of head — seemed to turn the prairie black.

1

The Oregon Trail was like a rope with both ends frayed. At one end were the "jumping off" places like **Independence** and **St. Joseph** in Missouri, and **Council Bluffs** in Iowa. At the other end, the trail divided to go to **Oregon**, **California**, or **Utah**. The first part of the trail took the pioneers across the flat tallgrass prairie of **Kansas** and **Nebraska** where the thick, tough grass grew taller than a man!

Missouri River

Fort Laramie

Mormon Trail

Council Bluffs

IOWA

N. Platte River

Scotts Bluff

Chimney Rock

NEBRASKA

Oregon Trail

St. Joseph

KANSAS

Independence

MISSOURI

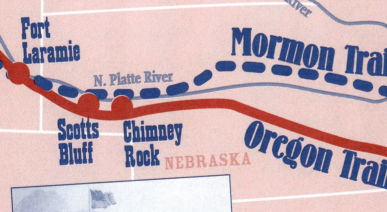

CROSSING INDIAN TERRITORY

The Oregon Trail cut through the center of Indian country. Some Indian nations like the *Mandan* (MAN–dan) and *Pawnee* (paw–NEE) had been on the plains for hundreds of years, living in villages and growing corn and other crops. The Pawnee even had built lodges out of logs covered with earth and grass.

Other Indian nations like the Fox, the Sauk, and the Shawnee had been displaced more recently. They were forced across the Mississippi onto the plains by white settlers or by other tribes. The *Cheyenne* (shy-ANN) had been corn farmers in Minnesota when

Lakota Sioux warriors forced them onto the plains, where they led a nomadic life, following the buffalo.

So the plains were home to many different Indian nations. More than anything else on the trail, the pioneers were afraid of these Indians. Yet, until the mid-1850s, Indians rarely had bothered the wagon trains except to raid the livestock. (That's why wagon trains would circle at night. They formed a portable corral for the animals.)

Some nations were friendly and traded with the wagon trains. Other nations demanded "tolls" in the form of tobacco, coffee, or sugar

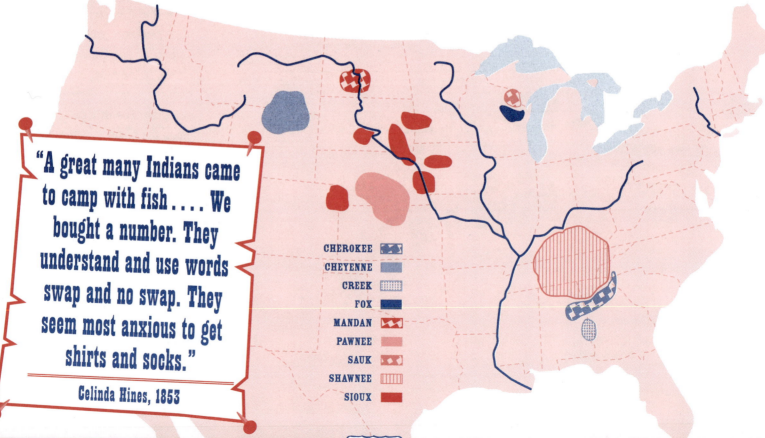

"A great many Indians came to camp with fish .... We bought a number. They understand and use words swap and no swap. They seem most anxious to get shirts and socks."

Celinda Hines, 1853

CHEROKEE
CHEYENNE
CREEK
FOX
MANDAN
PAWNEE
SAUK
SHAWNEE
SIOUX

to cross the land or rivers. If the emigrants cooperated, there would be no trouble.

Then, in 1854, an army officer from Fort Laramie made a thoughtless mistake. A cow had wandered away from a Mormon wagon train into a Sioux village. The Mormons reported the loss; the officer and soldiers went to retrieve the cow. The soldiers started a fight that led to their deaths, as well as the deaths of many Indians.

This incident started 36 years of fighting between Indians and the U.S. Army on the plains. After this battle, Indians started attacking wagon trains and settlers more often as they found themselves defending the open lands against what surely must have seemed like an invasion by the white man.

> "There is a toll bridge kept by the Indians across this stream. The toll for our team was six bits (75 cents). We have had some calls this evening from the Indians. We gave them something to eat and they left."
>
> Lydia Allen Rudd, 1852

Think About It!

Do You Believe Everything You Hear?

Many pioneers feared Indians more than anything else about traveling the trail because of all the frightening stories they had heard back East about dangerous Indians. Most of the stories weren't true or were wildly exaggerated, but they planted the seeds of fear and mistrust.

The real problem with rumors is that they change with every retelling, and even when proven untrue, they leave a negative impression. This is called "planting the seeds of doubt." How might you stop a rumor, and how can you be sure not to begin one? It's something to think about because with rumors, everyone is a loser!

❈ A DAY ON THE TRAIL ❈

Along the first stretch of the trail across Kansas to the Platte River, most days were uneventful. That is if you can call going places you've never been before, seeing strange animals and plants for the first time, crossing rivers on rafts, and hunting buffalo uneventful! Even so, there was a routine to most days, just like there is a routine to most days today.

"My (oxen) team leaders' names were Thom and Joe. They were more intelligent than many a man. Thom was my favorite and best and most willing and obedient servant and friend."

Joseph F. Smith, age 9

YOU ARE THERE

❧ After the Wagon Train ❧

All but five of the families on our wagon train still have their wagons and at least some supplies left. We have hardly any food left, and our shoes have holes in them, but we're all alive and well. Ma's best china is somewhere back on the trail, along with the other leeverites. The milk cow and Old Sal, one of the oxen we bought in Independence, both died of exhaustion on the Barlow Road. The remaining oxen will fatten up as soon as they get some rest and

eat some good grass in the valley. Pa figures we'll keep two oxen for plowing and sell the others to folks who've lost theirs. We'll use that money to buy seed, apple tree seedlings, and some livestock next spring. Yes, we're going to be apple growers here in the Willamette Valley! With the money we have left (about $100), we'll buy supplies. But things cost a lot here. Pa's worried there might not be enough for everything we need.

The folks who lost everything on

the trail will be OK, too. Ma says not to worry. Some of them have family living here already; others will stay in Oregon City for the winter, working at odd jobs or at the mills before setting out for their land. One boy about Ben's age who lost his ma and pa in a river crossing will live with us 'til he's old enough to claim his own land. It'll be a big help to have another pair of strong arms when it comes time to build our log cabin. Just like on the trail, everybody here seems ready to help each other.

YOU ARE THERE

Pa's Decision

Pa decided we have enough time before deep winter sets in to build a log cabin and enough money for supplies to see us through the winter. So we've bought everything we need and loaded up the wagon, and now we are on our claim along the Willamette. It's farther away from Oregon City than Ma had wanted, but there's a settlement about 10 miles (16 km) away, and Pa says the land's got deep, rich soil. There's a small meadow that we'll probably farm first. Most of the land is covered with tall fir trees, but we've found a small grove of oak trees in one corner.

We'll use the fir for our log cabin, says Pa, and for firewood. Cutting the trees and clearing the land sure will be hard, but we'll all pitch in and get the job done. Not even Pa seems worried, so I'm not either.

Paper Tricks!

Can you see through paper? Of course you can't. But the pioneers could. No, they didn't know magic, but they did know a clever trick. To let in some light before they could afford windows in their Oregon Country log cabins and their plains-styled sod homes, the clever pioneers devised their own paper "windows."

Try It! *Get a brown paper bag, a paper towel, and salad oil (the pioneers used lard). Cut a piece about the size of a napkin out of the paper bag. Using a paper towel, rub some oil onto one half of the brown paper. Flip it over and rub the same half on the other side.*

Hold the paper up to the light. Which half lets more light through? It's still not like a real window, but until windows were bought, oiled paper was a good substitute.

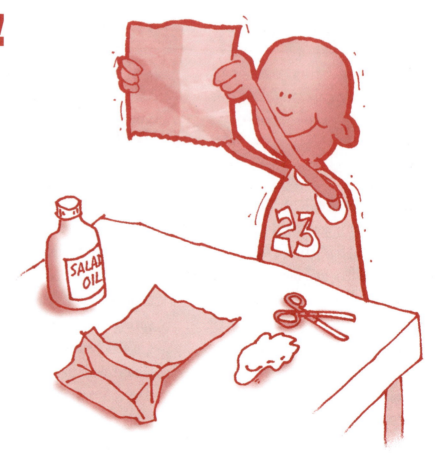

RIGHTS FOR WOMEN

Does it seem like Pa has made all the big decisions on the journey west? Women in the United States had few rights in the mid-1800s. They couldn't vote, sign contracts, or own land in most states. But the West helped change some of that. In Oregon, a law gave every married man who was either white or part white–part Indian a free parcel of land, but half of it had to be put in his wife's name. In California, for the first time, a married woman was allowed to keep whatever property she earned or acquired. And women got the vote for the first time in the West, in the Wyoming Territory, in 1869. It would take another 50 years for the United States to give women the right to vote in national elections.

The West often offered women more legal rights and personal freedoms than the eastern states or the federal government did. Why? Perhaps it had to do with the kind of people who went west or the jobs that pioneer women often had that were considered men's work. Or, maybe those who made the trip west realized that the men and women contributed *equally* to the success of the journey.

The Chrisman sisters on Lieban Creek, Custer County, Nebraska, 1886

Think About It!

Fairness and Equality

Girls on the trail take care of their baby brothers and sisters and help their mothers prepare all the meals. They're as bone-tired at the end of the day as any of the boys on the wagon train.

Yet, they know full well that one day the boys on the trail will get to own land (whether they marry on not), and they'll get to vote — but not the women.

How would you feel as the one without the rights? Would you assume "that's just the way it is," or would you be angry? Do any of your friends feel unequal — for any reason — at home or in school?

Frolic with Your Friends

Chores don't exactly spell fun, do they? But if you do them with friends, you can turn work into a party. Pioneers called their work parties to build barns or pick crops "frolics."

Why don't you hold a frolic with a bunch of friends? Choose a cause like cleaning up the neighborhood park. Make a frolic snack and hold races, play tag, or dance afterward. Just remember the one frolic rule — the work comes first!

Popcorn balls were a favorite frolic snack. The pioneers used molasses, but this way is a little easier. **(Please get adult help for the cooking.)**

Supplies

Makes 16 popcorn balls.

- 60 caramel candies (unwrapped)
- 1/4 cup (60 ml) water
- Large saucepan
- Stirring spoon
- 1 gallon (4 L) popped corn in a large bowl
- Waxed paper

1. Put the caramels and water in the pan over medium-low heat. Keep stirring until the candy is melted and the mixture is smooth.

2. Ask a grown-up to pour the mixture over the popcorn. Careful! It's very hot! When cool, wet your hands with water to keep things from getting too sticky. Shape the popcorn into balls.

3. *Put the balls on waxed paper and wait about an hour until they are firm. Put them in plastic bags if you want to keep them for a while or, better yet, pass them around to your frolicking friends! Yum!*

FRIENDS ACROSS THE BORDER

The United States and Great Britain were sharing the Oregon Country when Americans started pouring into it from the Oregon Trail. Americans eventually outnumbered the British and wanted it to be part of the United States. On June 15, 1846, with a few signatures at the bottom of a treaty, they got their wish. Britain took the northern part, which is now part of Canada, and the United States received the southern part.

The border set by the treaty is the same border that exists today. Few neighboring countries have such a long border between them. And few countries have lived side by side as friends for so long!

SPIRIT OF THE FRONTIER

YOU ARE THERE

I was just a kid when my family journeyed west on the Oregon Trail. I helped my family build a log cabin and carve an apple orchard out of the wilderness along the Willamette River. I grew up, got married, and had kids of my own. Now, here I am in 1893, reading a newspaper article that says the government has declared there is no more frontier. Hard to believe. Seems like there's still plenty of open land in the West.

But wait. The wilderness is gone. I can remember seeing buffalo herds on the prairie along the Oregon Trail. Now there are almost none. And I sure do remember my first train ride from the big lake to that city with all those pigs. Why, for a long time now, folks have been able to ride the rails clear across the country, easy as pie. This wild land's been tamed alright. Everywhere you go, you see farms and ranches, towns and cities, roads and railroad lines. The telegraph reaches from east to west, from north to south. Some western cities even have those newfangled telephones and electric lights!

The West positively hums with industry. On the prairie, farmers use steam-powered machines to harvest large crops of wheat and corn. They raise huge numbers of cattle, pigs, and sheep. They feed our own great nation and others, as well. In the mountains, big mining operations produce tons of iron ore for the steel industry and copper for the electric industry. Lumber companies supply the country with building materials. Yes-sir-ee, the government's right: The frontier is gone.

New Frontiers

Is the frontier really gone? Even today, more than a century later, some would say that the frontier still exists. A little bit of it is in every person's heart and mind and character. It's in free peoples' attitudes that it's OK to reach for the stars and want a better life. It's in the sense of optimism and the can-do spirit that North Americans are famous for all around the world. And it's in their determination and stubbornness, their belief in the individual, and their love of freedom. It seems that the frontier is as much a state of mind or an idea as it is an actual piece of land or place.

Places to Visit

Ash Hollow State Park, Lewellan, Nebraska
Chimney Rock National Historic Site, Bayard, Nebraska
Conner Prairie Museum Center and Prairietown Village, Fishers, Indiana
Donner Memorial State Park and Emigrant Trail Museum, Truckee, California
End of the Oregon Trail Interpretive Center, Oregon City, Oregon
Erie Canal Museum, Syracuse, New York
Fort Laramie National Historic Site, Fort Laramie, Wyoming
Genesee Country Village and Museum, Mumford, New York
Independence Rock, 48 miles south of Casper, Wyoming
Jefferson National Expansion Memorial/Museum of Westward Expansion, St. Louis, Missouri
McLoughlin House National Historic Site, Oregon City, Oregon
National Frontier Trails Center, Independence, Missouri
National Historic Oregon Trail Interpretive Center, Baker City, Oregon
Oregon Trail Museum/Scotts Bluff National Monument, Gering, Nebraska
Pioneer Farm Museum, Eatonville, Washington
Sutter's Fort State Historic Park, Sacramento, California
Tallgrass Prairie Preserve, Nature Conservancy, near Pawhuska, Oklahoma
Teton Wagon Train & Horse Adventure, Jackson, Wyoming
Three Island Crossing State Park, Glenns Ferry, Idaho
Trinidad History Museum, Trinidad, Colorado
Western Historic Trails Center, Council Bluffs, Iowa

Resources for Kids

Campbell, Maria. *People of the Buffalo: How the Plains Indians Lived.* Firefly Books, 1995.
Cobb, Mary. *The Quilt–Block History of Pioneer Days, With Projects Kids Can Make.* Millbrook Press, 1995.
Erickson, Paul. *Daily Life in a Covered Wagon.* Penguin US, 1997.
Fisher, Leonard Everett. *The Oregon Trail.* Holiday House, 1990.
Freedman, Russell. *Children of the Wild West.* Clarion Books, 1983.
Harness, Cheryl. *The Amazing Impossible Erie Canal.* Macmillan Books for Young Readers, 1995.
MacDonald, Fiona. *First Facts about the American Frontier.* Peter Bedrick Books, 1996.
Sandler, Martin W. *Pioneers.* A Library of Congress Book, HarperCollins Publishers, 1994.
Schlissel, Lillian. *Black Frontiers: A History of African American Heroes in the Old West.* Simon & Schuster Books for Young Readers, 1995.
Schlissel, Lillian. *The Way West: Journal of a Pioneer Woman.* Simon & Schuster, 1993.
Steedman, Scott. *A Frontier Fort on the Oregon Trail.* Peter Bedrick Books, 1993.
Stefoff, Rebecca. *Children of the Westward Trail.* The Millbrook Press, 1996.
Stefoff, Rebecca. *The Oregon Trail in American History.* Enslow Publishers, Inc., 1997.
Wadsworth, Ginger, editor. *Along the Santa Fe Trail: Marion Russell's Own Story.* Albert Whitman & Company, 1993.

Websites

End of the Oregon Trail	*www.endoftheoregontrail.org*
Erie Canal Online	*www.syracuse.com/features/eriecanal*
The Cherokee Trail of Tears	*www.rosecity.net/tears*
Fort Laramie	*www.calcite.rocky.edu/octa/ftl.htm*
The Gold Rush	*www.isu.edu/~trinmich/home.html*
Jefferson National Expansion Memorial / Museum of Westward Expansion	*www.nps.gov/jeff/main.htm*
National Road Association of Illinois	*www.nationalroad.org*
Oregon–California Trails Association	*www.octa-trails.org*
The Oregon Trail	*www.isu.edu/~trinmich/oregontrail.html*
Santa Fe National Historic Trail	*www.nps.gov/safe/fnl-sft/webvc/vchome2.htm*
Three Island Crossing	*www.wvi.com/users/TIC/tic.htm*

INDEX

M

N

O

P

R

S

T

W

MORE GOOD BOOKS FROM WILLIAMSON PUBLISHING

KALEIDOSCOPE KIDS® Books

Where Learning Meets Life
**96 pages, two-color, fully
illustrated, 10 x 10,
$10.95 US, ages 6 to 13**

Parents' Choice Recommended
**BRIDGES!
Amazing Structures to Design, Build & Test**
by Carol A. Johmann and Elizabeth J. Rieth

American Bookseller Pick of the Lists
Children's Book Council Notable Book
Dr. Toy 10 Best Educational Products
**PYRAMIDS!
50 Hands-On Activities to Experience Ancient Egypt**
by Avery Hart & Paul Mantell

American Boolseller Pick of the Lists
Children's Book Council Notable Book
**KNIGHTS & CASTLES
50 Hands-On Activities to Experience
the Middle Ages**
by Avery Hart & Paul Mantell

American Bookseller Pick of the Lists
Parent's Guide Children's Media Award
**ANCIENT GREECE!
40 Hands–On Activities to Experience This
Wondrous Age**
by Avery Hart & Paul Mantell

American Bookseller Pick of the Lists
**MEXICO!
40 Activities to Experience Mexico Past and Present**
by Susan Milord

**GEOLOGY ROCKS!
50 Hands-On Activities to Explore the Earth**
by Cindy Blobaum

**THE BEAST IN YOU!
Activities & Questions to Explore Evolution**
by Marc McCutcheon

**WHO <u>REALLY</u> DISCOVERED AMERICA?
Unraveling the Mystery & Solving the Puzzle**
by Avery Hart & Paul Mantell

Visit Our Website!

To see what's new at Williamson and learn more about specific books, visit our website at:

www.williamsonbooks.com

Or, call 800-234-8791 for a catalog.

TO ORDER BOOKS:

Williamson books are available from your favorite bookseller, or directly from Williamson Publishing.

☞ Toll-free phone orders with credit cards:
**1–800–234–8791
Visa or MasterCard accepted.**

☞ Or, send a check with your order to:
**Williamson Publishing Company
P.O. Box 185
Charlotte, Vermont 05445**

☞ E-mail orders with credit cards:
order@williamsonbooks.com

Catalog request: **mail, phone, or e-mail**

Please add **$3.20** for postage for one book
plus **50 cents** for each additional book.

Satisfaction is guaranteed or full refund
without questions or quibbles.

*Prices may be slightly higher when
purchased in Canada.*

Kaleidoscope Kids® is a registered
trademark of Williamson Publishing.